Nature Walk

Take a nature walk through the cool, dark woods to the pond. Move quietly and look closely. You never know what you might see.

Take a nature walk across
the hot, quiet desert.
It looks empty, but it's not.
Move slowly and take a closer
look. You may be surprised by
what you see.

Take a nature walk through the swamp.
Hot, humid air presses down. Sit motionless.
There's a lot to see.

Reptiles and Amphibians

Do you say "Yuck" when you touch a toad? Do you scream when you see a snake? You are not the only one who does this. Many people feel the same way about these animals. Most of the time people are afraid because they don't know much about them. This book will help you learn more about these misunderstood creatures. You may even learn to like them!

Connect the dots to find which animal is hiding here.

Reptiles

Reptiles are usually alike in these ways:

1 Most have four legs (except for snakes, of course).

2 They are covered with scales or body plates.

3 Most lay eggs which have a leathery skin.

4 They are cold-blooded.
This means a reptile's body stays the same
temperature as the air or water around it.

In cold climates where the winter temperature falls very low, most reptiles hibernate in a hole or rock crevice.

Look closely at these reptiles.
Can you see the scales or plates on each one?
Put an X on the reptile that lived long, long ago.

Turtles

Turtles are reptiles.
They are alike in these ways:

1 They have bony or leathery shells.

2 They have 4 legs and a short tail.

3 They lay eggs.

There are water turtles and land turtles.
A tortoise is one type of turtle that lives on land.
Wherever they live, they are interesting animals.

Some land turtles can pull their heads, feet, and tail inside their shells for protection. Water turtles have flatter, smoother shells for swimming. They cannot pull into their shells.

Turtles don't have any teeth. The front part of a turtle's mouth is like a hard bill. It lets them tear plant and animal food apart. Most turtles eat insects, worms, grubs, shellfish, fish, and some plants. A few kinds eat mostly plants.

Sea turtles return to the beach where they were hatched to lay their eggs. Other water turtles crawl up on the land to lay their eggs, too. Even when they are very small, turtles are strong swimmers.

Land turtles lay their eggs in holes in the ground. The mother turtle leaves in the nest. When the baby turtles dig out of the nest, they must take care of themselves.

There Are Many Kinds of Turtles

The snapping turtle has very strong jaws. It bites so hard that its jaws make a snapping sound.

The Galapagos tortoise is giant-sized. This tortoise can be as long as 5 feet (1.5 meters). It has big, thick legs to carry its heavy shell.

The green turtle has a smooth, flat shell. Its legs are shaped like flippers for swimming. It lives in the sea.

The spotted turtle is only about 4 inches (10 cm) long. It lives in places with still, fresh water. It only eats when it is in the water.

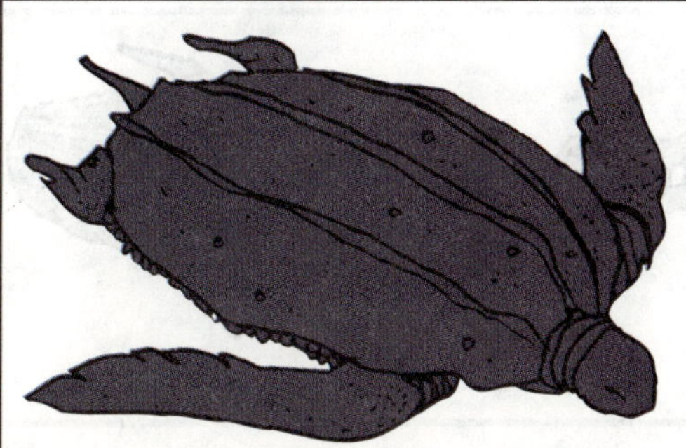

The leatherback turtle is the biggest sea turtle. It can be over 8 feet (2.4 meters) long. It has a leathery shell with ridges.

Circle the biggest land turtle.
Put an X on the biggest sea turtle.

Crocodilians
(croc-uh-DILL-ee-uns)

Alligators and crocodiles are crocodilians. Crocodilians are reptiles. Crocodilians are alike in these ways:

1. They have large scales.
2. They have 4 legs.
3. They have long snouts with sharp teeth.
4. They lay eggs.

Crocodilians are the largest living reptiles. Saltwater crocodiles can get as big as 20 feet (6 meters) long. Crocodilians live where water and land come together. They live where the weather is warm. Most crocodilians live in fresh water. A few kinds live where rivers run into the sea. In these places the water is salty. Crocodilians are often found in swampy areas.

Crocodilians have tough skin. It is made of scales that fit beside each other. They have strong jaws and a powerful tail.

Crocodilians are meat-eaters. They wait quietly in the water until they see something tasty to eat, then they move quickly. Almost anything that moves is food to crocodilians. Their young eat insects, snails, and other small animals. Adults eat larger animals such as deer or zebras that come too close to the water. They drag the animal into the water and drown it.

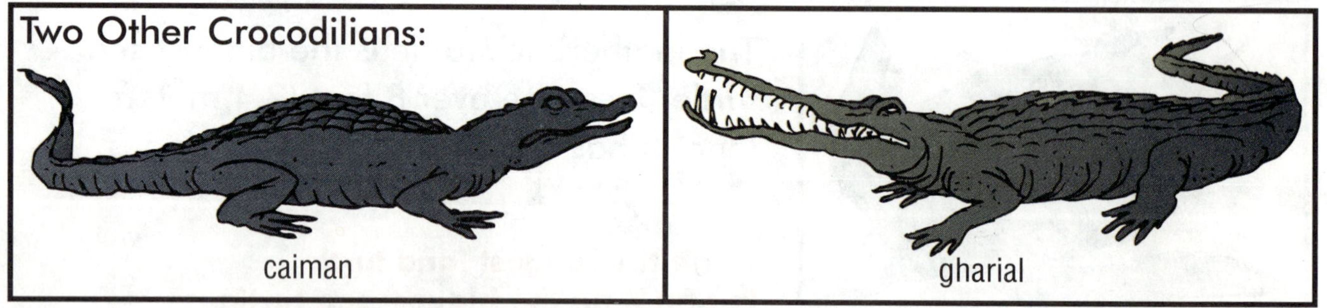
Two Other Crocodilians:

caiman

gharial

More About Crocodiles and Alligators

Both crocodiles and alligators have long, scaly bodies. They have four legs and a long tail.

A crocodile has a long lower tooth that shows when its mouth is closed. It has a long, thin snout.

An alligator has a rounder snout. It does not have a lower tooth that shows.

Both alligators and crocodiles eat fish, turtles, birds, crabs, and other water life.

Both crocodiles and alligators lay eggs with a hard shell. Crocodiles lay their eggs in nests they dig in the ground. Alligators lay their eggs in nests they build out of mud, grass, leaves, and branches. They build their nests above the ground.

Whose nest is it?

Snakes are reptiles. There are many kinds of snakes. Snakes are alike in these ways:

1 They have scales.

2 They don't have legs.

3 They have loose skulls and big mouths.

4 They do not have eyelids.

Some snakes lay eggs. Some snakes have live babies. Snakes come in many different sizes, shapes, and colors.

The emerald tree boa uses its color to hide among leaves and branches.
Color this snake so it can hide in these leafy plants.

EMC 4105

More About Snakes

Snakes use their tongues to collect smells. They take these smells into their mouth to give them information. They find out if danger is near. They find out if food is near.

Snakes rub off their skin when it gets too tight. This is called molting.

Snakes can open their mouths very wide. They can even swallow something wider than their own head. They swallow their food whole. It is crushed inside the snake's body.

Some snakes squeeze their prey until it is dead. Poisonous snakes use venom (poison) to capture prey.

The shortest snake in the world is a thread snake. It can be as small as 4 1/4 inches (10.8 cm).

The longest snake in the world is a kind of python. It can be 33 feet (9.9 meters) long.

Lizards

Lizards are reptiles.
Lizards are alike in these ways:

1 They have horny, smooth, or beaded skin.

2 Most lizards have 4 legs.

3 They have claws on their toes.

4 Most lay eggs.

Lizards lay in the sun in the morning and in the evening to soak up heat. They stay in the shade during the hottest part of the day.

Most lizards eat insects and other small animals. There are a few kinds that eat plants. Lizards watch for something moving. This is how they see their prey. Then, as quick as lightning, they take off and catch it. Most lizards can run very fast and most can swim.

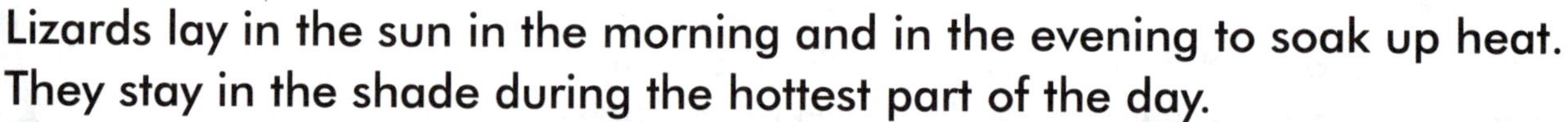

A gila monster is one type of lizard that is slow and clumsy. It is also poisonous. Once it catches its prey it takes a bite and hangs on. Gila monsters eat eggs, mice, and other lizards.

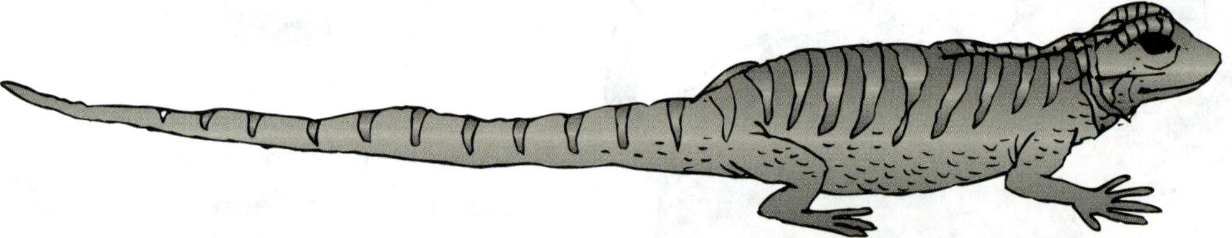

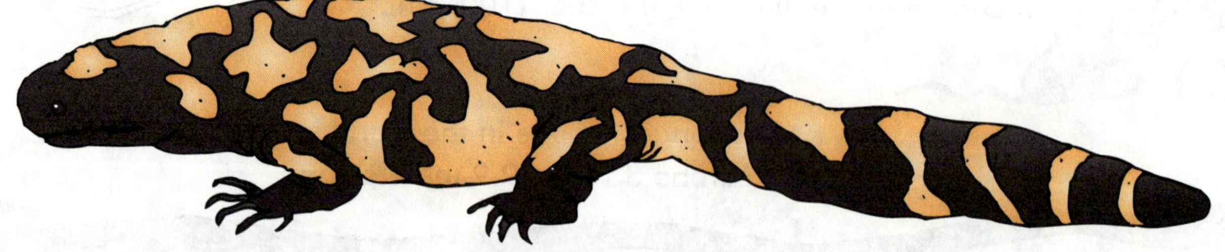

Geckos have large pads on their toes to help them climb. They eat small insects and live around houses or in trees.

The anole and chameleon lizards can change color for camouflage.

Horned lizards look a lot like toads. They have flat, bumpy bodies. They have spines on their heads.

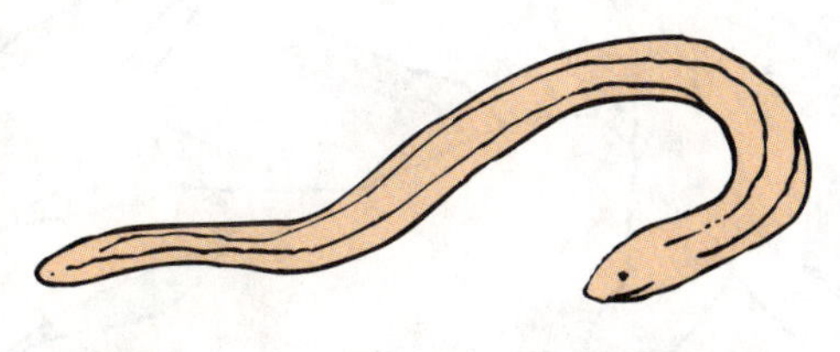

Worm lizards burrow underground. They have no legs and look a lot like big earthworms.

A komodo dragon is a huge lizard. It can be 10 feet (3 meters) long.

Tuatara

The tuatara is a reptile. There is only one kind of tuatara. It lives in New Zealand.

A tuatara:

 has scales

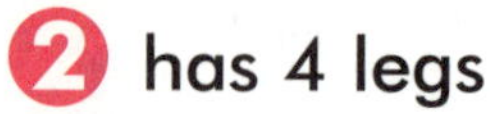 has 4 legs

3 lays eggs

A tuatara is about 2 feet (60 cm) long. It has sharp teeth and a crest from its head down to its tail.

The tuatara lives in burrows. It comes out at night to eat worms, small lizards, young birds, and insects.

A female tuatara digs a hole in the soil to make a nest for her eggs. Tuatara babies grow very slowly. They will not be grown for 20 years.

Unusual Reptiles

Use this code to find the names of the strange reptiles.

1 - a	5 - e	9 - i	13 - m	17 - q	21 - u	25 - y
2 - b	6 - f	10 - j	14 - n	18 - r	22 - v	26 - z
3 - c	7 - g	11 - k	15 - o	19 - s	23 - w	
4 - d	8 - h	12 - l	16 - p	20 - t	24 - x	

I look fierce when I am attacked.

_f_ __ __ __ __ __ __
6   18   9   12   12   5   4

__ __ __ __ __ __
12   9   26   1   18   4

Some people call me a toad, but I am really a lizard.

__ __ __ __ __ __
8   15   18   14   5   4

__ __ __ __ __ __
12   9   26   1   18   4

I give you a warning if you come too close.

__ __ __ __ __ __ __ __ __ __ __
18   1   20   20   12   5   19   14   1   11   5

I live in the ocean, but I lay my eggs on the beach.

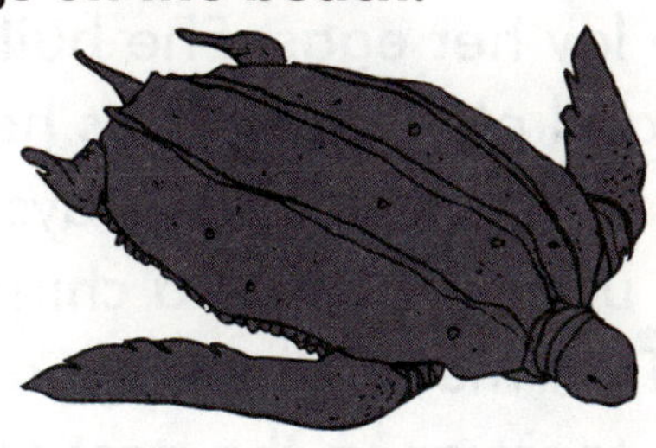

__ __ __ __ __ __ __ __ __ __ __
12   5   1   20   8   5   18   2   1   3   11

__ __ __ __ __ __
20   21   18   20   12   5

Reptile Life Cycles

A few reptiles give birth to live babies, but most lay eggs.

This sea turtle spends her life in the sea until she is ready to lay her eggs. She crawls up on the same beach where she was hatched. She digs a hole in the sand and lays her eggs. After she covers her nest with sand, she crawls back into the sea. When the babies hatch, they must dig their way out of the nest and crawl to the sea.

This alligator lives in a swamp. She crawls up on the bank when she is ready to lay her eggs. She builds a nest of mud and plants. She lays her eggs and covers them up. She stays around the nest until she hears a chirping sound. That means the eggs are hatching. She tears open the nest so the baby alligators can get out. The alligator is the only reptile that takes care of its young. She will look after them until they are larger and can take care of themselves.

Sea Turtle and Alligator Life Cycles

Number the steps in these life cycles.
Answer the questions yes or no.

Sea Turtle

1. The mother sea turtle digs a hole in the sand.   yes   no
2. A mother sea turtle takes care of her babies.   yes   no
3. The babies crawl into the sea after they hatch.   yes   no

Alligator

1. A mother alligator digs a hole for her eggs.   yes   no
2. A mother alligator takes care of her babies.   yes   no
3. The babies make a noise when they are hatching.   yes   no

Look at the pictures in this book if you need help.

Draw the reptile that can pull its head and legs into its shell.

Draw the reptile that has a long snout and tail and lots of sharp teeth.

Draw the lizard that looks like a toad with spines.

Draw the reptile that has no legs but can still move fast.

We Are Amphibians

Frogs, toads, and salamanders are all amphibians.
They are alike in these ways:

1. Adults usually have four legs.
2. They have smooth or warty skin. It is usually moist.
3. They don't have claws.
4. They lay jelly-like eggs in the water.

Most amphibians live in or near water.

Baby amphibians are born in the water. When they hatch they look more like fish than frogs, toads, and salamanders. They breathe with gills. They change a lot as they grow up. They grow legs and lungs.

Most amphibians hide and sleep during the day. They come out at night to look for food.

Amphibians are cold-blooded. If it is warm, they are warm. If it is cold, they are cold. When it is too hot, amphibians find shade or go into the cool water. When it is too cold, they lay out in the sunshine to soak up heat.

If it gets really cold in winter, amphibians find a place to hide. Their breathing slows down. Their hearts almost stop beating. They stay this way until the weather is warm again.

**I am a caecilian (suh-séel-yun).
I am an amphibian, too.**

Frogs and Toads

Frogs and toads are alike in these ways:

1. They have short, round bodies.
2. They have large, strong back legs.
3. They do not have tails when they grow up.
4. They have big, bulging eyes.
5. They don't have necks.
6. They spend part of their life in water and part on land.
7. They lay jelly-like eggs in water.

Frogs and toads are different in these ways:

1. A toad is fatter than a frog. It has rough, bumpy skin. It is damp, but not wet. A toad lives on land. It is not as quick as a frog.

2. A frog has smooth, wet skin. It lives in or near water. It moves quickly.

Circle the frogs.
Put an X on the toads.

Answer These Questions

Am I a frog or a toad?

I live on land except to lay eggs. I am a ___________________________.

I live in or near the water. I am a ___________________________.

I have bumpy skin. I am a ___________________________.

I have smooth skin. I am a ___________________________.

I am the fatter one. I am a ___________________________.

I move faster. I am a ___________________________.

Where does it live?

Different kinds of frogs have different kinds of feet:

Frogs that live in water have feet with webs to help them swim.

Frogs that burrow underground have pointed toes to help dig in the soil.

Frogs that live in trees have sticky pads on their toes. This helps them hang on to branches and leaves.

Match:

More About Frogs and Toads

Frogs and toads are meat-eaters:

They eat insects and worms. Some even eat smaller frogs and toads. Big bullfrogs will even eat small turtles, snakes, mice, and birds.

Frogs and toads come out at night to hunt for food. They have to see something move to know it is food. If an insect or worm is still, it is safe from a hungry frog. But as soon as it moves even a little bit, out comes a long tongue to grab it.

Frogs and toads are protected in many ways:

Some hide in the water with just their eyes sticking up.

Some use color to hide. A green frog in a green tree is hard to see.

Some puff up to a large size to frighten their enemies.

Some are poisonous. These frogs and toads can be very colorful. Their bright colors warn other animals to stay away.

Some use their strong legs to hop away from danger.

Salamanders

Salamanders are amphibians.
They are alike in these ways:

1. Their front and back legs are about the same size.
2. They have tails.
3. They have smooth skin.
4. They lay jelly-like eggs without shells.
5. They lay their eggs in water.

Newts and sirens are kinds of salamanders, too.

Some salamanders live in the water all the time. Some live on moist land. All kinds lay their eggs in water.

Salamanders breathe with gills when they are babies in the water. Some salamanders breathe with lungs when they are grown. Some never grow lungs.

The mudpuppy is one kind of salamander that keeps its fluffy gills all of its life.

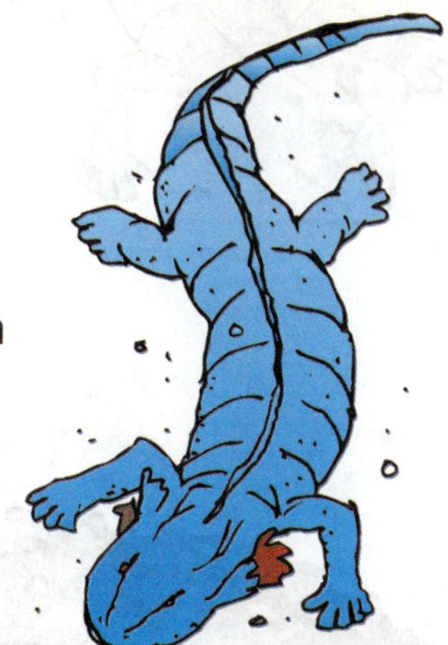

The red salamander gets oxygen through its skin.

The fire salamander breathes with lungs.

Salamanders are meat-eaters. Some kinds eat insects, worms, and snails. Some kinds eat small fish, crayfish, and eggs. Some kinds even eat mice.

Frogs, Toads, and Salamanders

Circle the frogs and toads.
Underline the salamanders.

Amphibian Life Cycles

Frog

The mother frog lays her eggs in water. They look like balls of jelly with black dots in the middle. When they hatch, the baby frogs have a round body and a long tail. They are called tadpoles. Tadpoles don't look like frogs at all. They breathe with gills.

First tadpoles grow back legs. Then they grow front legs. As their bodies grow, their tails get smaller and smaller. Their gills go away and they grow lungs. Before long they look like just like frogs, only smaller. They will keep growing until they are as big as their parents. Then they can hop up on the land.

Tiger Salamander

The female salamander lays her eggs in the water. When salamander babies hatch, they already have legs. They breathe with feathery gills. The little salamanders eat and grow. They get bigger and begin to look like their parents. Their gills go away and they grow lungs. They will keep growing until they are as big as their parents.

Some salamanders go on land when they are grown. Other salamanders stay in the water their whole life.

Frog and Salamander Life Cycles

Number the steps in these life cycles.
Answer the questions yes or no.

Frog

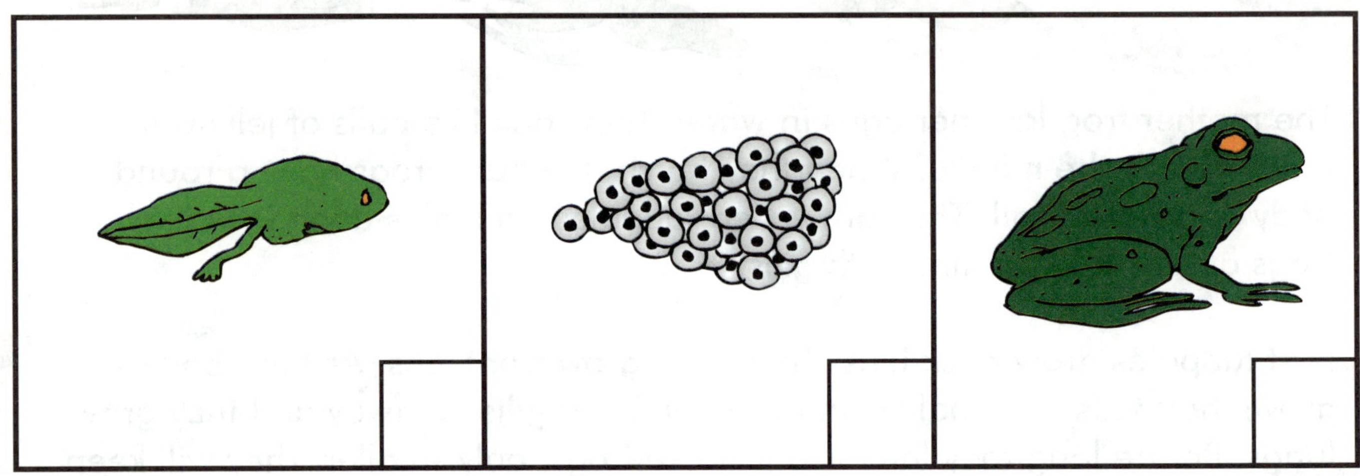

1. Frogs lay eggs with hard shells.   yes   no
2. Tadpoles look like frogs.   yes   no
3. Tadpoles breathe with gills.   yes   no

Salamander

1. When salamanders hatch they have legs.   yes   no
2. Salamanders build nests of twigs.   yes   no
3. A baby salamander breaths with gills.   yes   no

Read the riddles.
Look at the pictures.
Cut and paste the answers with the riddles.

1. I am long and black. I have 4 tiny feet. Who am I? paste	2. My skin is bumpy. Who am I? paste	3. I have 4 legs, but no tail. I am small and green. Who am I? paste
4. I have 4 legs and a tail. I am green with spots. Who am I? paste	5. I have big, round spots on my body. I have a long tail. Who am I? paste	6. I don't have a tail. I have spots on my smooth skin. Who am I? paste

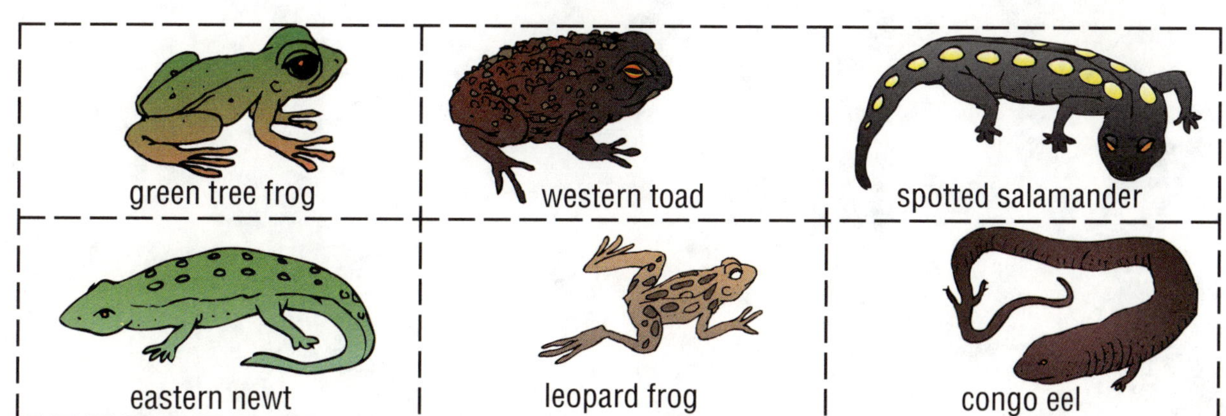

Egg to Frog

Parents: You will need to supervise the collection of frog eggs.

Look around the edges of a pond where plants are growing. When you find some eggs, scoop them carefully into a jar. When the frogs are grown, return them to the pond.

You need:

- large bowl or aquarium tank
- algae-covered rocks
- pond water, mud, and small plants
- frog's eggs or tadpoles

1. Place rocks, mud, and plants in the aquarium.
2. Add enough pond water to fill the bowl or tank about half full. Put in a large rock that reaches **above** the level of the water. (The frogs will need a place to come out of the water to breathe once they have lungs.)
3. Put in the frog eggs or tadpoles. **Do Not Change The Water!**
4. The young tadpoles will eat the algae and small green plants. Older ones can be fed raw ground beef or chopped worms.
5. Watch as they grow and change. When they get four legs, look out!

Make a Hopping Frog

Parents: You may need to help your child with these folding directions.

**You will need scissors and crayons to make this hopping frog.
Cut out the page and fold your frog by following these directions.**

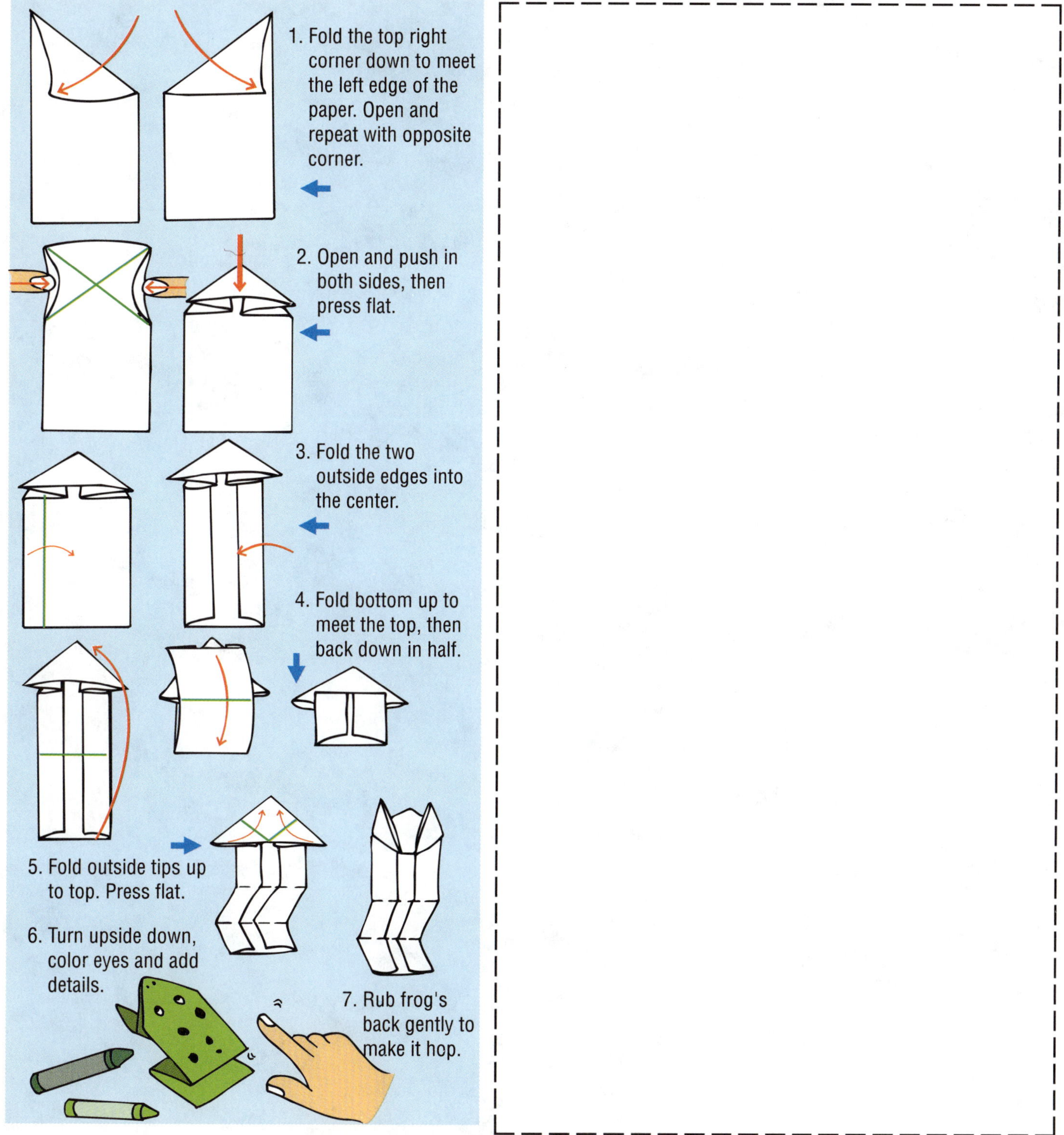

Amphibian and Reptile Word Search

```
m u d p u p p y c h i c k
t u r t l e d o g s i t s
k p c r o c o d i l e o a
i g u a n a b o x i n r l
n u t s l i z a r d o t a
g i l a m o n s t e r o m
s a s s y s u g a r g i a
n e w k i n s a a t e s n
a l l i g a t o r i c e d
k i t n o k i s s p k t e
e g g k u e f r o g o o r
n e w t h o r s e t o a d
```

<table>
<tr><td rowspan="4">W O R D   B O X</td></tr>
</table>

WORD BOX			
alligator	gila monster	mudpuppy	slider
crocodile	iguana	newt	snake
frog	kingsnake	salamander	toad
gecko	lizard	skink	tortoise
			turtle

Answer Key

Please take time to go over the work your child has completed. Ask your child to explain what he/she has done. Praise both success and effort. If mistakes have been made, explain what the answer should have been and how to find it. Let your child know that mistakes are a part of learning. The time you spend with your child helps let him/her know you feel learning is important.

page 4

page 5

page 7

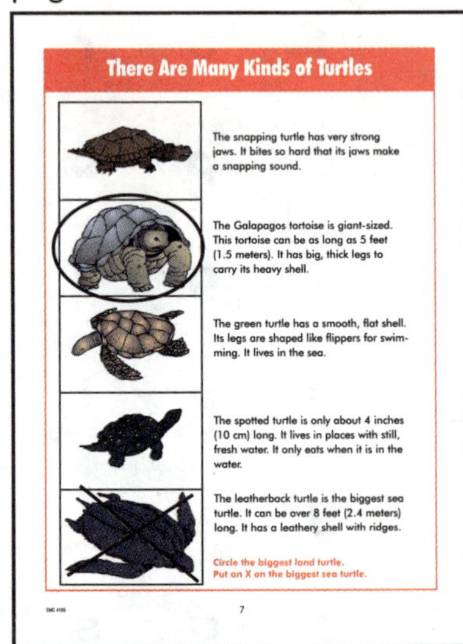

page 9

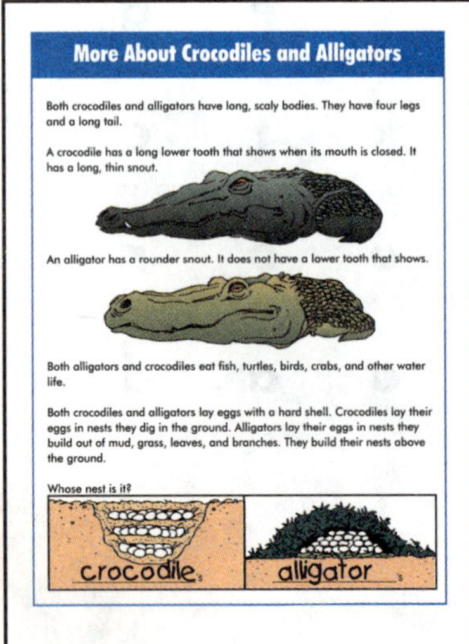

page 15

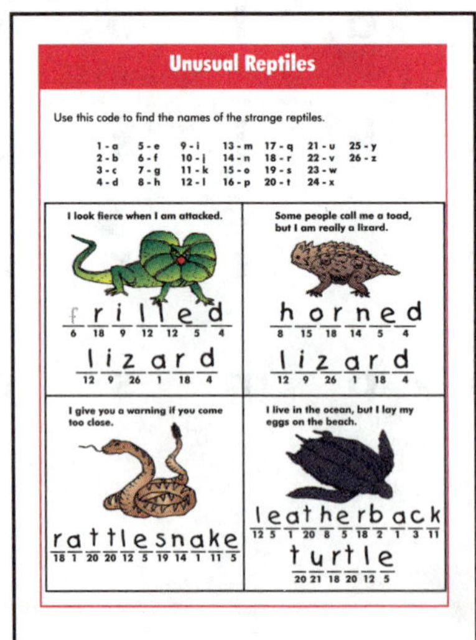

page 17

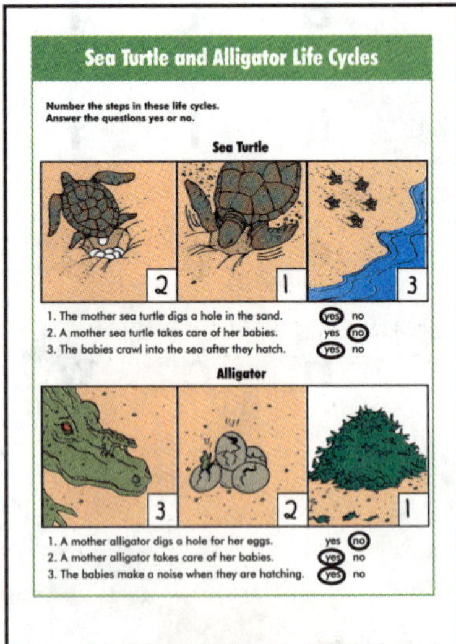